Also by Frederick Seidel

AREA CODE 212

LIFE ON EARTH

THE COSMOS POEMS

GOING FAST

MY TOKYO

THESE DAYS

POEMS, 1959–1979

SUNRISE

FINAL SOLUTIONS

T0057959

THE COSMOS TRILOGY

THE COSMOS TRILOGY

Frederick Seidel

FARRAR, STRAUS AND GIROUX
NEW YORK

Farrar, Straus and Giroux

18 West 18th Street, New York 10011

Printed in the United States of America
First edition, 2003

The poems in this collection, with the exception of poem 100,
were originally published by Farrar, Straus and Giroux
in three separate volumes: *The Cosmos Poems* (2000),
Life on Earth (2001), and *Area Code 212* (2002).

Library of Congress Cataloging-in-Publication Data
Seidel, Frederick, 1936–
    The cosmos trilogy / Frederick Seidel.— 1st ed.
        p.   cm.
    ISBN 0-374-52891-8
    I. Title.

PS3569.E5A6 2003
811'.54—dc21

                                            2003049053

Designed by Peter A. Andersen

www.fsgbooks.com

CONTENTS

THE COSMOS POEMS

1	Into the Emptiness	3
2	Mirror Full of Stars	5
3	Who the Universe Is	7
4	Universes	9
5	Black Stovepipe Hat	11
6	The Childhood Sunlight	13
7	Beyond the Event Horizon	15
8	Blue and Pink	17
9	Galaxies	19
10	Feminists in Space	21
11	This New Planetarium	23
12	Invisible Dark Matter	25
13	A Twittering Ball	27
14	The Star	29
15	Special Relativity	31
16	Take Me to Infinity	33
17	Poem	35
18	Supersymmetry	37
19	Everything	39
20	Happiness	41
21	The Eleven Dimensions	43
22	The Royal Palm	45
23	Faint Galaxy	47

24 Edward Witten   49

25 The Birth of the Universe   51

26 Starlight   53

27 Quantum Mechanics   55

28 It Is the Morning of the Universe   57

29 Forever   59

30 Forever   61

31 Forever   63

32 The Last Remaining Angel   65

33 In the Green Mountains   67

LIFE ON EARTH

34 Bali   71

35 French Polynesia   73

36 The Opposite of a Dark Dungeon   75

37 Star Bright   77

38 Goodness   79

39 Joan of Arc   81

40 Doctor Love   83

41 Fever   85

42 Blood   87

43 Holly Andersen   89

44 At New York Hospital   91

45 Drinks at the Carlyle   93

46 Chiquita Gregory   95

47 To Start at End   97

48 We Have Ignition   99

49 Eternity   101

50 The Master Jeweler Joel Rosenthal   103

51 In Spite of Everything   105

52 Springtime   107

53 Summer   109

54 Fall Snowfall   111

55 Christmas   113

56 Cosmopolitans at the Paradise   115

57 Sex   117

58 Song   119

59 The Seal   121

60 Her Song   123

61 Green Dress, 1999   125

62 Letter to the Editors of *Vogue*   127

63 James Baldwin in Paris   129

64 St. Louis, Missouri   131

65 Hamlet   133

66 Frederick Seidel   135

AREA CODE 212

67 I Do   139

68 The Bathroom Door   141

69 Downtown   143

70 The Serpent   145

71 Getaway   147

72 Nothing Will   149

73 pH   151

74 Venus   153

75 Nigra Sum   155

76	Rain in Hell	157
77	Dido with Dildo	159
78	January	161
79	February	163
80	In Cap Ferrat	165
81	March	167
82	Easter	169
83	April	171
84	May	173
85	Venus Wants Jesus	175
86	MV Agusta Rally, Cascina Costa, Italy	177
87	June	179
88	June Allyson and Mae West	181
89	July	183
90	Hugh Jeremy Chisholm	185
91	August	187
92	September	189
93	The Tenth Month	191
94	Fall	193
95	October	195
96	November	197
97	God Exploding	199
98	The War of the Worlds	201
99	December	203
100	One Hundred	205

THE COSMOS POEMS

INTO THE EMPTINESS

Into the emptiness that weighs
More than the universe
Another universe begins
Smaller than the last.

Begins to smaller
Than the last.
Dimensions
Do not yet exist.

My friend, the darkness
Into which the seed
Of all eleven dimensions
Is planted is small.

Travel with me back
Before it grows to more.
The church bell bongs,
Which means it must be noon.

Some are playing hopscotch
Or skipping rope during recess,
And some are swinging on swings,
And seesaws are seesawing.

That she is shy,
Which means it must be May,
Turns into virgin snow
And walking mittened home with laughing friends.

And the small birds singing,
And the sudden silence,
And the curtains billow,
And the spring thunder will follow—

And the rush of freshness,
And the epileptic fit that foams.
The universe does not exist
Before it does.

MIRROR FULL OF STARS

A can of shaving cream inflates
A ping-pong ball of lather,
Thick, hot, smaller than an atom, soon
The size of the world.

This does take time to happen.
Back at the start
Again, a pinprick swells so violently
It shoots out

Hallways to other worlds,
But keeps expanding
Till it is all
There is. The universe is all there is.

Don't play with matches.
The candle flame follows her
With its eyes. The night sky is a mirror
On a wall.

What she stands in front of are the roaring afterburners
Of the distant stars a foot away
Leaving for another world. They have been summoned
To leave her

For another girl
In another world who stands there looking
In a mirror full of stars
At herself in her room.

The room is not really,
But it might be. If there is
Something else as beautiful
As this snow softly falling outside, say.

The universe begins
With a hot ball of lather expanding
In a hand
That should be in her bed asleep.

WHO THE UNIVERSE IS

The opposite of everything
That will be once
The universe begins
Is who it is.

Laws do not apply
To the pre-universe.
None of it
Does not make sense.

Puffs to the size
Of an orange in one single stunned
Instant
From smaller than a proton.

Morning coffee black
Happiness so condensed
Had to expand to this,
Had to expand to this,

Had to expand to this
Universe of love
Of freezing old
Invisible dark matter

To give it gravity.
If the hot unbelievable
Nothingness feeds
Itself into a hole and starts,

None of this does not make sense
Once you understand
The stars are who it is,
The sisters and the brothers.

Set the toaster setting between Light and Dark
And the unimaginable
Pre-universe will pop up a slice of strings
In eleven dimensions which balloons.

UNIVERSES

Think of the suckers on the tentacles
Without the tentacles. A honeycomb
Of space writhing in the dark.
Time deforming it, time itself deformed.

Fifteen billion light-years later a president
Of the United States gives the Gettysburg Address.
Two minutes. The solar system
Star beams down on him.

Other special stars express themselves,
Not shy at all, particles
Of powder floating on the swirl, each
Vast—each a vast pillow covering

A hidden speck it murderously
Attempts to suffocate.
The speck will eat it up.
The speck of gravity is a hole.

Through that hole there is a way.
There are as many of these, there are as many of these
Invisible black caviar
Specks as it would take

To fill the inside of St. Peter's to the roof.
It is the number
Of grains of sand on the shores
Surrounding the continent of Africa times ten.

Each invisible eyelet is a black hole
Highway out of time.
Think of the universe as a beanbag
On a bobsled on a run under lights at night.

Inside are universes.
It is incompletely dark inside.
There is motion.
There is the possibility.

BLACK STOVEPIPE HAT

The wobbly flesh of an oyster
Out of its shell on the battlefield is the feel
Of spacetime
In the young universe.

The petals of the rose
Of time invaded
The attitude of zero and made it
Soften its attitude.

Lincoln's black stovepipe hat
Was dusty when he sat down
To scant applause. Many in the crowd did not know
He had just delivered

The Gettysburg Address, but it is over,
And the stars keep on redshifting,
The universe keeps on expanding
The petals of the rose.

U. S. Grant's cigar's red tip
Pulsed the primal fireball out
Through the new universe
It was the creator of with shock waves.

Speckles of the stars
And baby's breath (the flower)
Activate infinity
And decorate the parlor.

Baby's breath is counting on the roses
With it in the vases.
It is difficult to understand
Why the universe began.

It is difficult to be
Robert E. Lee.
Why does the cosmos have to happen?
What is another way?

THE CHILDHOOD SUNLIGHT

Blessed is the childhood sunlight
The solar star emotes.
Darkly filled-up emptiness
And galaxies too far away

Are what we feel inside ourselves
That make us want to walk somewhere,
And then we run and jump and sing.
The universe is not enough,

We rock 'n' roll to other ones
Through black hole wormhole timeways,
But here right now the rain has stopped,
The air is warm.

The parking lot washed clean smells sweet,
And even has a rainbow that
A little girl tiptoes toward,
Hoping not to frighten it.

The neighbor's dog that won't go home
Is watching her—which she can't see—
With naked eyes of love and awe.
She feels that way herself sometimes.

When you are sure that you're alone,
Tell yourself to not be sure.
This universe is not the first.
The other ones are not the same.

Or anyway no one can know.
At night when she should be asleep
She lights a match and blows it out
To show she has the power to.

Computers crunch the numbers and
The other stars lie down and say
The sun exhausts itself with light.
So good night.

BEYOND THE EVENT HORIZON

And isn't it
The presence of a thing
That can't be seen
More massive than the universe?

And isn't it the strings
Of its own gut beneath infinity the bow
Who vibrate musically to make
The Primal Scene?

You realize this means
The massless spin-2 particle whose
Couplings at long distances
Are those of general relativity.

It means
Strings of an instrument that are
Ten to the minus thirty-two centimeters
In diameter in the Theory of Everything.

It means the temple
Is of a size
Too small for belief—indeed, whose
Dimensions do not begin.

O instrument.
O scene that moves the bow.
We could be everything that
Could be otherwise,

Reversed inside the tiny walled whirlpool
Of a black hole, but can't.
Even infinity is stuck and can't stop.
We could be

Playing with the toys
In another space,
Generating the video
Of something else.

BLUE AND PINK

The very young universe has reached
The size of a BB.
The idiopathic
Rheostat dialed up the expansion.

Suddenly it sticks out
A hair of spacetime.
It is of course the size of the universe
Inside the tiny BB.

All this happened long ago,
But still is happening
In my mind as I look for the runway
In the fumes.

Oxygen
Is not in the atmosphere
Of this particular planet.
The mother-of-pearl means that

If we decide to land,
We will slide. The ammonia park
Is the innocent summer's day
Colors of a Della Robbia terra-cotta statue.

The oil derrick-like devices pumping
Are the creatures.
We do a flyby
And decide better not.

Baby blanket blue and baby blanket pink we were warned
To watch out for when we were launched.
The good ship *Gigabyte*
Sails the seas of space.

Girls and boys, every planet we visit is different.
Some are made of ice cream and some are the blue and pink
Of the sign in front of the movie star's house:
ARMED RESPONSE.

GALAXIES

Everyone knows that the moon
Is made of rice,
But how many of you know
That the jellyfish

You see in the picture on page 8—
Everybody open your book—
Is eleven million light-years wide?
It is beautiful, to boot.

It is beautiful to kick
The ball into the goal.
It is beautiful to know how
To answer the phone.

The jelly that looks like frog spawn
You see in the back pond
Is so many stars.
No, stars are different from Mars.

Everybody come to the window.
The blackness of space
Is simply the everything we are,
Subtracting the light.

The everything we are,
Minus the light,
Is what the battery acid is
Without the bulb.

But the bulb without the lens
To focus the heart
Is the spaceship we are all in
Without the artificially created gravity we need.

We all need
Our mothers and fathers who are dead.
We all need to be good
In case we will die too.

FEMINISTS IN SPACE

The stars are happy flowers in a meadow.
The grass is green and sweetly modest.
The burble of the brook
Is the thrust powered back.

Best friend, you walk with me through life,
Let's take a walk in space.
I'm suiting up, not easy, lots of laughter,
Squirming out of the girl suit, floating into the other.

We will be feminists in space,
Flying toward the stars,
With our backpack portable life-support,
All a grownup needs,

Even if there is a tether back to the mother
Ship we came from.
Leave your dolls behind.
Opening the hatch.

Two gentlemen are out taking a stroll
In their space suits big as polar bears.
That blue-eyed snowball is the planet Earth.
Oh, there's America, my earth, my ground.

Cars and factories and rain forests burning have farted
The cloud-cover that suffocates the ball,
Which up here we jet away from
With our jet-nozzles, squirting around like squids.

We can do anything we want.
We can turn somersaults all day long.
I also want to star in a movie but I want to sing
By being a scientist and being my brain.

Women of the world unite
Already at ten years old.
Two friends are skipping home from school,
Each with her own thoughts.

THIS NEW PLANETARIUM

The universe roars an expletive
Starburst in every direction
Like the U.S. Navy Blue Angels
Flying their routine.

Everyone talks about the silence of light
But no one talks about the sound
Beyond decibels that
Is equally uncontainable,

And which the heavens declare the glory
Of as the jets explode
In joys expanding at a rate
That is increasing.

It is the candles
On a birthday cake blowing out
But lighting up — it is after the fast
A feast of spacetime

Faster and faster, uncontainable,
As the whole thing breathes out,
The rib cage of the universe expanding
Quite a bit faster than at the beginning.

Everyone talks about the silence
But no one talks about the sound.
I hear the light.
I hear the mighty organ bellowing heaven through

The bars of my playpen and I
Stand up, wobbling, age one,
Holding on to the sunshine
That is falling outside my window.

The light roars through this new planetarium.
Most of the universe is
The dark matter we are not made of,
But we stand.

INVISIBLE DARK MATTER

It is the invisible
Dark matter we are not made of
That I am afraid of.
Most of the universe consists of this.

I put a single normal ice cube
In my drink.
It weighs one hundred million tons.
It is a sample from the densest star.

I read my way across
The awe I wrote
That you are reading now.
I can't believe that you are there

Except you are. I wonder what
Cosmologists don't know
That could be everything
There is.

The someone looking at the page
Could be the everything there is,
Material that shines,
Or shined.

Dark matter is another
Matter. Cosmologists don't know.
The physicists do not.
The stars are not.

Another thing beside
The row of things is
Standing there. It is invisible,
And reads without a sound.

It doesn't matter
That it doesn't really.
I need to take its hand
To cross the street.

A TWITTERING BALL

A twittering ball of birds
Repeatedly bursts in the sky,
Losing its shape but regaining it,
Making a fist and unfolding finger by finger

Time and galaxies and dust
Out of the little beginning herpes
Pimple swelling
Energy out, heat, huge,

Spacetime hiccuping
Itself outward into
Itself in exponential surges
According to the mathematics.

The mathematics prepares
The student stars.
It predicts a certain
Unevenness in the performance.

How to connect the very small
To the very large is the task
Ahead. The task ahead
Is the path of the mathematics not yet

Walked down to the place
Where we meet in a mirror,
Sit down together, raise a glass of wine
And smile, nodding in accord.

General relativity
And quantum theory at the same table at last
Lift a fork
The size of the universe to eat a pea.

The Planck length is the pea.
Hawking guiding his self-powered wheelchair
And Einstein riding his bicycle
Walk the Planck.

THE STAR

I was thinking about dogs
To fight death.
They get hold of it by the teeth and can
Go on forever.

Their eyes are pure
Fame and purity.
This was just an idea.
It came from thinking about the star.

I don't know its name.
It is very far away.
What does it say?
I was walking down by the water.

The night was warm,
The smell of spring.
In outer space the cold
Is fertile and freezes anything clean.

The star has the face
Of a flower.
It is burning and freezing
Immensity.

It has the power
To say a name.
When you look out the specially reinforced viewhole
Of the spaceship at the universe,

You are glancing down at the top
Of a tee as you prop a golf ball there
For the drive.
You look off in the distance toward the flag.

The black velvet lining of the box
That holds the stars is soft.
I let the dogs off the leash
And let them run and I pray.

SPECIAL RELATIVITY

I am pushing the hidden
Pedals of my little car
To get somewhere I have
To get to.

The stars are everywhere, like tourists
At cherry blossom time.
A mist of cosmic dust
Drifts by for years.

Little Red Car to Earth:
I am up here. It's fun.
I'm doing all the things.
I'm signing off now to pedal.

The little boy pedaled
Through space in his car.
The birch canoe paddled
To avoid the black hole.

The stars stared,
Not being cool,
And stalked the celebrity cherry
Blossoms for an autograph.

And the very latest,
And the weather forecast,
And the Weather Channel,
And motorcycles are dangerous.

I was furiously pumping
The pedals of my little car
To get somewhere I had
To get to.

By the laws of special relativity,
I began to wrinkle and bend.
The universe has no end,
But I am getting there.

TAKE ME TO INFINITY

We are completely
In the dark with our eyes.
We listen with the radio
Telescope to the noise.

We repair the Hubble
Telescope in place in space because they hiss
It is head and shoulders above a 200-inch dish
On a mountaintop — but really

Astronomy is just like
Playing in the bath with a rubber duck
And looking at the universe all
At once and

We know so much nothing,
Why not know some more?
I say to the people
Of the United States,

Enough time has passed.
I say to the people of the world,
The time has come
And gone and now.

How did the universe begin?
I will count to ten.
How will it end?
I had the most amazing dream.

You were on all fours like a dog
And I was walking you
Around —
And you were me!

And I was reading me the riot act
Because I don't make sense.
Both of me say: Take me to infinity!
Take me to before the universe!

POEM 17

Her hobby is laughter.
She plays the musical saw.
Her bunk is aft.
It's her turn to sleep.

Mission Control is working feverishly
Through the night
To solve the problem and needs her
Awake.

The international space crew
Floats in the dark
Composing final thoughts
And smelling the smoke.

She is the most popular
Mission Commander
In the history of the Shakespeare program ever—
Brave, Chinese, and brilliantly alive.

She is a wife and mother
And Girl Scout leader.
Suddenly the ship shakes violently.
Something has exploded.

Shakespeare 5 has been sent up
With all the world's hopes. One
Last chance to deflect the asteroid.
This is Mission Control. We're not reading you, *Shakespeare*. Over.

She wakes up in her crib
And is covered with moonlight.
She hears the nearby murmur
Of voices

Which must be the TV
One billion human beings
Are watching.
Someone softly covers her with her blanket.

SUPERSYMMETRY

You step into the elevator
To go down and it goes up,
And the surprise
Of the sensation of sudden

Happiness is weightless.
So is love.
The chemistry of intergalactic
Space is scarcely human,

But on the other hand we
Are all related.
So is love.
Einstein bicycled right here, didn't he?

The guru Edward Witten, talking
Along the same Princeton streets many years after
And into the grounds of the Institute
For Advanced Study, is not lost.

He zooms to a blackboard
Of equations about
The quantum mechanics
Of the central thing when it is raining outside.

He titters behind
The flutter of a geisha fan,
In heavy makeup, left, right, male, female,
Kabuki, kooky.

Over the ocean in France, the platinum meter stick
Under a glass bell is rational,
And meaningless,
And dissolving.

But Witten grasps it cheerily in one hand
And the geisha fan in the other,
Like the pots of gold at the ends of the rainbow
In the rain.

19
EVERYTHING

And they overwhelm you and force
You to stay still till it is over.
Movies do.
I like the speed of light.

I like the speed
And the incomparably blurred
Sensation of being deformed
Into being and about to begin.

The starter is the inexhaustible
Appetite of the non-living
Miracle to grow a universe, so to speak,
So many digits

Every blink,
Tick tick tick tick
From the beginning.
I unlock the steamer trunk

From the days when they used to
Travel with steamer trunks. I lift the lid and inside
Find the original blast of spacetime
Growing outward toward a distant shore.

The stars are singing to the stars
In there, stars to stars.
It isn't over
When the galaxies cluster

And the audience is crying
And you are.
It overwhelms you and forces
You to stay till it is over.

The same poem over and over
You are witnessing, the swelling of the universe
Into the rose
Which it will give.

20 HAPPINESS

It isn't every day, but most,
That one inflicts this on oneself.
It is intolerable.
Such universality

Means there is no other place
So one must do it here, do
And be, and feel the joy
Most days bring.

We have scars
On our imagination that come from
Joy. I mean, the woman has
A huge star sapphire buried

In the middle of her forehead, yes?
And that is good.
And the universe she sits
On is.

Her third eye is.
However, it bleeds.
The universe is in a skillet
Cooking into something yum.

I say
Cimabue painted her without the sapphire
Holding the infant Jesus.
The dervish dancers swirl

In their white robes which whirl the stars
Into galaxies and the galaxies
Into cheese. The blue shoe is the Earth
Seen from space,

And its blade twirls on the ice of the skating rink
In the dark. There is no point
In trying to think about this
Bliss.

THE ELEVEN DIMENSIONS

The images received are
One light-year old.
That has been confirmed.
On the monitor is

A wide boulevard of black
Lacquer in a capital.
A faint fuzz
Of spring blur coats the trees.

The headlights on in the rain must be
Their eyes.
The trees are the dogs
We know so little about

That they walked.
We have no idea what
Language they used
And did they use their mouths to excrete

What then was
Capitalized
To produce the malt
Which reproduced the songs?

They knew there were
More than three dimensions
To their wives.
Every year they called it spring.

They practiced herd individualism
And ran alone together.
Every headlight drank an evening cocktail
And didn't drive.

They knew there were
Eleven dimensions,
Which they didn't know
Were about to begin.

THE ROYAL PALM

The tiny octopus
Of galaxies and dust is
The universe taking up
Space.

The octopus also is
The black space around itself
Its octopus ink
Clones in clouds.

Its round human eye is looking
Out at nothing.
Its eight tentacles
Are fingering ink-jet spacetime.

It squirts the self
Around itself it floats in.
It opens its eight arms wide.
It opens its eye and mouth and suckers wide.

It is an eight-armed dome and does.
It is the universe and is.
It is the Royal Palm
Of consciousness slightly swaying above the beach.

Angels are swimming
In the sea.
Manta rays ripple by
Nearby.

The interstellar dust
Keeps incubating life.
The oral
Sharks are always having fun.

One tank at the aquarium
Of nothingness
Contains all this
Zest.

FAINT GALAXY

I come from
Far away from you
And that is
Far away.

Hundreds of
Millions of stars in a
Galaxy and billions of galaxies and one
Billions of light-years away.

I came from
Far away from you
And that was
Far away.

My news is billions
Of light-years ago. When
I started to come toward
You.

And somewhere
Along the way. I
Forget
What I was going to say.

I came from
Far away from you and
That is far
Away.

The light
That reaches you now
Is I
Began far off.

That touches your eyes.
That enters your thought.
From afar.
From the start.

EDWARD WITTEN

Witten is designing
A baby's bib
With a little red
Sea horse raised

Embroidered emblem. Now
When baby spits out the baby food paste
The universe is spooning into her face
A little red sea horse will catch it.

A little red
Sea horse is eleven-dimensional
Spacetime. It unicycles
Upright in space

In all directions
At once.
A little thread sea horse
Is deaf,

Blind, can't smell,
Has no voice.
The universe
Is also raised

On a background of something else,
And the something else
Is there to catch something
Else.

It will catch hell
For the unfathomable inhuman
Daring of the theory
The heroic Edward Witten

At the Institute for Advanced Study
Has put forward in the Theory of Everything
To the effect
That we spill.

THE BIRTH OF THE UNIVERSE

The perfect petals
Of the rose
Of time, of all three
Angels that prepare for this,

Of everything the blue
Warm water does
To magnify the August hour,
The perfect

Thunder mint
Between the thumb and finger
Makes, or the large smell of rain before it rains,
Grow from several storm cells

Violently,
While the hour
Hand sweeps as if it were barking seconds
And the day stands still,

In perfect bloom,
And so the universe
Was just conceived,
And just arrives,

And jets a rising fountain
Lit with many lights
And colors,
And a rushing sound,

And it is night,
And it is air,
And the ice cream is infinite
Above the cone

The small hand holds
Dripping, holds the torch
Of everything
Is good.

STARLIGHT

To return to the impossible
Is to be happy in the future
With what after all was the start
And continues to produce.

You know what that means?
It means you are in love.
It means to live your life
You have to.

The universe is ourself
Moving in sleep
Very slowly or in sudden
Seizures toward eternal life.

The universe is a single organism
Made of two
Or more individual,
Or many more than two, individual

Moving parts and blitzkrampf,
Explosive but balletic slow-mo
Of vast organs
Of ecstasy making sounds

The radio telescopes will hear
Billions of light-years from now,
The way whales croon
Whalesong through the ocean microphone

To an audience in darkness far away.
To live your life
You have to use it up.
A star performs its nuclear core.

Beautiful Kate Valk of the Wooster Group
Of actors does the male title role in *The Emperor Jones*
In blackface till she is so much
Starlight she stops.

QUANTUM MECHANICS

It is raining on one side
Of the street and
A mother on the other.
Boy, it's hot!

Incandescence not making sense,
The ultimate
The weather will
Allow.

Of the energy
Of a supernova the
Undertow
Collapses to,

It has been said
There is no way to
Express the utterly
Unlighted

Out the other side.
It can appear out of nowhere
Outside your own front door.
Knock, knock.

Come in. It's open.
Delivery!
Come in, it's open.
Fifteen billion light-years is fast food

To the divine quantum equations
It is delivered to —
Which eat the delivery boy,
According to Heisenberg.

They have charm
And quark and spin.
They work both sides of the street.
They give good infinity.

IT IS THE MORNING OF
THE UNIVERSE

It is the morning of the universe:
Black children on their way to school to read.
The storefront metal gates on rollers rise
And all the shops are open now for praise.

It's hard to bear the beauty.
The traffic is sweet this early.
The old are up and listen,
Though the ones who don't get up don't listen.

Even in a universe this young
Things ask why
Enormous stars blow up
And more stars are born.

Born to burn,
They start to cry.
The young stars burn and shine.
That's the law.

As for the mania of being always
On,
It consumes the nuclear core
And beams truth through space

As deeply as a child reads his first real book.
When they assemble the biggest telescope ever
On the far side of the skin,
They will be able to see

A boy not moving his lips
And a book being read,
Free of the wobbles
Of earth atmosphere distortion.

Stars collide and explode
And their young are born.
The children arrive at school.
A billion years go by.

The innocence of the tornado
Of the universe torridly
Twists the universe, the way a clay pot turns
On a potter's wheel languidly

Gaining form, the funnel and the rapturous
Waist swaying slowly
Like a belly dancer at ten million
Miles an hour, sways like an elephant's trunk

Of clots of rough and gray indigestible
That will be stars
And galaxies and strum and strums
The invisible cold dark matter,

Earsplitting odorless suction coming
Through time that stands
On its tail and the other force,
And is everything

Filling space,
And is space and everything,
Spacetime, everything.
What are we?

The everything looks
Out without eyes.
What are we?
Between everything and no.

The cobra sways
To the music
The belly dancer sways
To and the urge.

Gravity sings to the other force
And the other force sings back.
The hypnotized body floats in the air.
Love is God.

FOREVER

The surge of energy death can't
Protect itself against
Imagines everything
At once.

The surge protector
That a spike of energy
Can't avoid,
And that the spike of energy

Destroyed,
Fires its last distress flare forever,
Which is the aftermath
Till now, and is this place.

There is the tendency
Not to be
Which required
A singularity

To overcome
It, which made a blast which
Imaged everything
Just once,

The flash forever
That the flare flashes
Forever.
One consequence of the disappearance

Of nothingness
Is all the bandages eerily
Unwind and soon
The pharaoh finds the energy inside

The mummy case to lift
The lid. The flash of the universe
Goes out
To the eyes of time.

FOREVER

I travel further than
I can to reach the place
I can. I reach
The place.

Stars testify.
The black is
Satisfied with that.
The black of space is old cold.

How cold it feels
When you remember warm.
I swim with winter wings
Beneath the Royal Palms.

Birth put a message
In a bottle and floated it away.
My DNA washed up on a shore, facelift smiling,
My plump green grape maturity flash-frozen.

I drank so much.
So many women
I touched.
The voyage to outer space parties forever.

The reading material is
Incinerated and
The mind gets so old cold
I ache but

Yes, those are stars.
Yes, in the vicinity of zero, the grape's now
Nearly fleshless face lifts
A trumpet to its lips.

American eternity
Swooningly crooning ballads on the red vinyl LP
From the 1950s on earth
Turns away wrath, swords into songs, undying rebirth.

THE LAST REMAINING ANGEL

Thinner than a fingerprint
And smaller than a postage stamp,
It looks like brains
Or softly scrambled eggs.

It moves in waves,
The latest Stealth technology.
It gets there fast.
The galaxies do the parallel processing.

Another miracle, the stars.
They give their lives when they fall.
The others pick up after them.
The implant keeps the bad things out.

It shocks the heart, restores the rhythm.
The operating system loves it.
The stars become so meek and mighty.
Sometimes things don't always crash.

A woman is a wingless angel flying.
The last remaining angel joined her.
The entire known universe
Is their high-wire act.

Everything there is is the trapeze, no net.
And now abideth faith, hope, gravity,
These three, but the greatest of these
Is the ground.

The universe is taking off
Its clothes and taking
Off in a hailstorm. The runway
Looks like brains. It looks like love

Is everything there is.
Things in boots
Are murdering the Jews on Mars
And other galaxies don't know.

IN THE GREEN MOUNTAINS

Into the emptiness that weighs
More than the universe
Another universe is born
Smaller than the last.

Good tidings of great joy.
Adonai.
Glory be to God in the highest and likewise
To those of us who don't believe.

For Buddha
Is the advice
Of the stand-up comic
Hooded cobra god of the young, serene.

Unleashing the nourishing rain,
My lord Monsoon lashes the delta.
They sing from the Torah
The beginning of the universe

At the young woman's Bat Mitzvah. Behold.
I bring you good
Tidings of great joy.
Adonai.

My friend, the darkness
Into which the seed
Of all eleven dimensions
Is planted is small.

That she is shy,
Which means it must be May,
Turns into green and June
And the seedling synagogue in Bennington.

And the small birds singing,
And the sudden silence,
And the curtains of the Ark billow open,
And the Tibetan tubas in the echoing Green Mountains roar.

LIFE ON EARTH

Is there intelligent life in the universe?
No glass
In the windows of the bus
In from the airport, only air and perfume.

Every porch in the darkness was lighted
With twinkling oil lamps
And there was music
At 2 a.m., the gamelan.

I hear the cosmos
And smell the Asian flowers
And there were candles
Mental as wind chimes in the soft night.

Translucency the flames showed through,
The heavy makeup the little dancers wore,
The scented sudden and the nubile slow
Lava flow of the temple troupe performing for the hotel guests.

Her middle finger touches her thumb in the *vitarkamudra*,
While her heavily made-up eyes shift wildly,
Facial contortions silently acting out the drama,
And the thin neck yin-yangs back and forth to the music.

Announcing the gods,
The room jerked and the shower curtain swayed.
All the water in the swimming pool
Trampolined out, and in the mountains hundreds died.

The generals wanted to replace Sukarno.
Because of his syphilis he was losing touch
With the Communist threat and getting rather crazy.
So they slaughtered the Communists and the rich Chinese.

Gentle Balinese murdered gentle Balinese,
And, in the usual pogrom, killed
The smart hardworking Chinese,
Merchants to the poor, Jews in paradise.

FRENCH POLYNESIA

Drinking and incest and endless ease
Is paradise and child abuse
And battered wives.
There are no other jobs.

Everything else is either
Food or bulimia.
The melon drips with this.
It opens and hisses happiness.

A riderless horse sticks out,
Pink as an earthworm, standing on the beach.
Fish, fish, fish,
I feel fishish.

I develop
When I get below my depth.
I splinter into jewels, Cadillac-finned balls,
Chromed mercury no one can grab.

I care below the surface.
Veils in
Colors I haven't seen in fifty years nibble
Coral.

Easter Sunday in Papeete.
Launched and dined at L'Acajou.
The Polynesians set off for outer space
In order to be born, steering by the stars.

Specialists in the canoes chant
The navigation vectors.
Across the universe,
A thousand candles are lighted

In the spaceships and the light roars
And the choir soars. A profusion
Of fruit and flowers in tubs being offered
Forms foam and stars.

THE OPPOSITE OF
A DARK DUNGEON

Three hundred steps down
From the top
Pilgrims are
Looking up.

The temple is above
In a cave.
The stairs to it start next
To the standard frantic street.

Monkeys beg on
The stairs
All the way
Up to the entrance.

Vendors sell treats
To the pilgrims to feed to them.
Some people are afraid of monkeys
Because they think they might get bitten.

When you finally reach the top, somewhat
Out of breath, you enter
The heavy cold darkness
And buy a ticket.

The twenty-foot gilded figures recline.
There are trinkets you can buy to lay at their smiling feet.
They use up the universe with their size.
Their energy is balm and complete.

Everything in the cosmos
Is in the cave, including the monkeys
Outside. Everything is
The opposite of a dark dungeon. And so

A messenger from light arrived.
Of course they never know that they're a messenger.
Don't know they carry a message.
And then they stay a while and then they leave.

STAR BRIGHT

The story goes one day
A messenger from light arrived.
Of course they never know that they're a messenger.
Don't know they carry a message.

The submarine stayed just
Below the surface with its engines off near the shore observing.
One day the world took off its shoes and disappeared
Inside the central mosque

And never came back out. Outside the periscope the rain
Had stopped, the fires on shore were
Out. Outside the mosque
The vast empty plaza was the city's outdoor market till

The satellite observed the changing
Colors of the planet
And reported to the submarine that
No one was alive.

A messenger from light arrived.
Of course they never know that they're a messenger.
Don't know they carry a message.
And then they stay a while and then they leave.

Arrived, was ushered in,
Got in a waiting car and drove away.
Was ushered in,
Kowtowed to the Sacred Presence the required ten times

And backed away from the Sacred Presence blind,
And turned back into light.
Good night,
Blind light.

Far star, star bright.
And though they never know that they're a messenger,
Never know they carry a message,
At least they stay a while before they leave.

38 GOODNESS

In paradise on earth each angel has to work.
Jean-Louis de Gourcuff and his wife spend hours
Spreading new gravel in the courtyard and the drive.
The château swan keeps approaching its friend Jean-Louis to help.

Monsieur le Comte et Madame la Comtesse
Have faith, give hope, show charity.
This is the Château of Fontenay.
And this is the Gourcuffs' ancient yellow lab, Ralph.

It's de rigueur for French aristocrats to name their dogs in English.
Something about happiness is expressed
By the swan's leaving the safety of its pond,
Given the number of English names around.

Ralph smiles and says *woof* and the swan smiles and says *hiss*
In a sort of Christian bliss.
What is more Christian than this?
You have entered the kingdom of the kind.

Old Count de Gourcuff lives in another wing, the father,
Tall big-boned splendor of an English gentleman, but French.
His small wife is even more grand and more France.
One has a whisky with him in the library.

Something about goodness is being expressed
At a neighbor's château nearby.
In the marble reception hall, ghosts are drinking champagne.
The host will be shot right afterward by the Nazis for something.

Blind Ralph barks at the hissing swan he waddles behind and adores.
It is left to the childlike to lead the sick and the poor.
Jean-Louis de Gourcuff, the saintly mayor of Fontenay,
Dons his sash of office, white, blue, and red.

Dominique de Gourcuff makes regular
Pilgrimages with the infirm, to refresh her heart, to Lourdes.
Dinosaurs on their way to being birds
Are the angels down here in heaven.

JOAN OF ARC

Even her friends don't like her.
Tears roll out of
Her tear ducts,
Boulders meant to crush.

She feels
Her own emptiness but oddly
It feels like love
When you have no insight at all

Except that you are good.
The tears crush even
That thought out and she is left happily
Undressed with her stupidity.

Nobody wants her
On their side in games at school
So the retard
Is wired to explode.

She smokes, gets drunk,
Gets caught, gets thrown out
As the ringleader when she was not since
She has no followers, this most innocent

Who is completely
Emptiness,
Who is a thrill no one wants and
Whom the cowed will kill.

The "Goddamns" (as the invading English are
Called) get in her France.
It made the Maid of Orleans a man and God
Hears her crewcut rapture screaming at the stake in pants.

For God's sake, the food is burning
On the stove!
You are the only one in the world.
You are my good girl.

DOCTOR LOVE

It was a treatment called
Doctor Love, after the main character.
One of the producers discovered
To our horror a real

Dr. Love who, eerily, by
Pure coincidence, was also a woman
Oncologist trying to identify the gene that causes
Breast cancer. My

Fiction trampolined
Herself right off the treatment page,
Landing not on a movie set or a screen at the multiplex,
But at a teaching hospital in Los Angeles directing

Her lab. If you could identify the gene
That turns the cancer on,
Then maybe you could find a way to turn it off—
And make somebody rich.

She found a gene.
The villain needed to learn which.
He sets the innocent doctor up to
Commit a murder. The story was in such bad taste.

It never made sense.
I was doing rounds in a long white coat
To write the screenplay—playing doctor, doctor love.
Till death us do part, Dr. Catharine Hart,

I will remember you
On the street kissing me hello.
The cherry blossom petals blow—
White coats on rounds

In a soft East River breeze—like glowing fireflies of snow.
Dear Hart, it is spring.
Cutting a person open
Is possible without pain.

FEVER

Your pillow is pouring
You like a waterfall
You sleep through
In the middle of.

You shiver sweat
In the middle of
The rain forest chattering in
Darkness at midday.

You like heat because
It makes a reptile warm.
On the raft with you
Is your life.

You have everything
You have.
The crocodiles choo-chooing around
And around are the snouts

Of your ancestors
Which split and jaggedly yawn
Because it is time to
Read aloud

The story
Of the African slaves walking on water
In chains all the way to the United States
In 1776.

Two hundred–plus years later,
Islam overthrows the Shah.
No Menstruation Women Allow,
A temple sign had said on Bali.

The temple monkeys had not been friendly.
The president of the rubber-stamp Iranian senate,
Sharif-Imami, the loathed Shah
Loved. The fever breaks.

42 BLOOD

The yellow sunlight with
The milky moonlight makes
An egg without cholesterol
And I will live.

O tree of brains
And sound of leaves.
The day is green.
And now I pray.

I thank the cotton
For the shirt.
I thank the glass that holds me
In, that I see through into out there.

I'm driving to the car wash
And the dogs are getting haircuts
And the motorcycles drive by
And I ask for mine,

My body in your hands
To live.
The bay is blue
To me means that.

The saline breeze says that
The soft is firm enough today
To hold the water up
With gulls on top that won't

Sink in.
I don't know when.
I don't know how.
I don't know I.

I tell the cardiologist that
I'm in love.
The needle draws the champagne
Into crystal flutes the lab will love.

HOLLY ANDERSEN

I describe you.
I have a chart to.
I hold your
Heart. I feel.

The motor
Of your life
Is not diseased or weak
Or real until

I stress it from the
Outside, how
You test anyone before you
Find them true.

Totally in
Your power,
The stethoscope
Puts its taproot to your chest, and flowers.

The miles of
Treadmill agnostically
Takes core samples.
The bolus which jump-starts us back to life is love.

The light leaps and is living
On the screen
As the mine-detector mechanism
Looks for mines.

Take a deep breath.
You stopped smoking cigarettes.
Breathe out through your mouth.
How many years ago.

We are made of years
That keep on living.
We are made of tears
That as your doctor I can't cry.

AT NEW YORK HOSPITAL

I enter the center.
I open the book of there.
I leave my clothes in a locker.
I gown myself and scrub in.

Anything is possible that I do.
Cutting a person open
Is possible without pain. An entourage rolls
In a murderous head of state with beautiful big breasts—

Who is already under and extremely nude
On the gurney. Her sheet has slipped off.
Her perfect head has been shaved
Bald. And now a target area

On the top of the skull will
Be painted magenta. Her body is re-wrapped.
Her face gets sealed off. Her crimes against humanity
Will be lasered.

I am a Confederate scout, silence in the forest.
The all eyes and stillness
Of a bird watcher has stumbled on
A Yankee soldier asleep.

The dentist's drill drills a hole and
The drill slips and whines out of control,
But no matter. The electric saw cuts
Out a skullcap of bone.

The helicopter descends from Olympus to within an
Inch of touching down
On the wrinkled surface, when a tool falls incredibly
To the floor and I pick it up and am thanked.

The anesthesiologist for my benefit joyously
Declaims Gerard Manley Hopkins.
The surgeon recites a fervent favorite childhood hymn.
He slaps the monster tenderly to wake her up. Wake up, darling.

DRINKS AT THE CARLYLE

The pregnant woman stares out the spaceship window at space—
But is listening carefully.
The man is looking at the inward look on her face.
The man is answering her question while they leave the galaxy.

Why they are on this space voyage neither stranger quite knows.
There is something that
Someone watching them
Might feel almost shows,

But would not be able to say what.
She was describing the American child
She was, the athlete who played the violin,
Who grew up on Earth upstate.

He sees American thrust, the freckled ignition
Who vanished in a puff of smoke on stage—and the power and
Grandly pregnant happily married woman physician
There on stage when the smoke cleared. He looks at her left hand

And her bow hand. He sees the child lift the half-size violin
From its case, and take the bow,
And fit the violin to her shoulder and chin,
And begin to saw, sweetly, badly,

While she asks him what it is like to be him,
To be a space commander, revered.
He stares softly at her severed
Connection to him as she again looks inward

And very distantly smiles
While he tries to think what she is asking him and answer.
She is smartly dressed in black,
Blond midnight in the air-conditioned hot middle of summer.

She has smilingly said she is the only doctor in town on
Fridays in July, so she knows everything.
It is amazing what people actually do.
I am not possible to know.

CHIQUITA GREGORY

Sagaponack swings the Atlantic around its head
Like an athlete in the windup for the hammer throw.
It is a hurricane and the radio
Predicts a tornado will follow.

The air violently
Smells fresh like nowhere else,
And I am just assuming it is
You calling to everyone lunch is ready.

We are heads bowed
At our place cards. Zeus is saying grace
When the chairs begin to shake and lightning outside
Shazams you back to life, tsunami

Light as a feather, the feather of life,
Very long legs,
Very short shorts, a chef's apron in front, so that from
Behind . . . Goddess,

You have returned to earth in a mood and
In a storm, and I have no doubt that
Irreplaceable trees on Sagg Main are davening
Themselves to the ground. They

Rend their clothes and tear their hair out out
Of joy. Chiquita, how can anyone be so
Angry who has died? The whirling light in
The drive is the police, here

To urge the last holdouts in houses near the
Ocean to leave. To help us
Decide, they suavely ask for the name of next of kin.
The ocean bursts into towering flames of foam.

The lobsters in the pot are screaming
Inside the reddening roar.
Your aproned ghost keeps boiling more, keeps boiling more,
And turns to serve the gore.

TO START AT END

To start at End
And work back
To the mouth
Is the start—

Back to the black hole
That ate the meal,
Back from the universe
And the book

To the illiteracy
Of the much too
Compressed pre-universe
To release. So it was

The hands of fingers on
The keyboard bringing up on the screen
The something thirteen
Billion light-years back that happened,

The *Gentlemen, start your engines!*
That made it start,
Which is the mouth
Of the music.

The uncontrollable
Is about to happen—
A gash in the nothingness invisibly
Appears.

The uncontrollable is about
To happen—the strings (of String Theory)
Are trembling unseen ecstatically
Before they even are touched by the bow.

It all happened so fast.
The fall weather was vast.
At either end of space-time the armies massed.
Youth was past.

WE HAVE IGNITION

Infinity was one of many
In a writhing pot of spaghetti.
One among many
Intestines of time.

The
Trembling the size and color
Of boiled lobster coral
Was trying

More violently than anything
Could and still live. The
Subatomic particles
Were

The truth. One of them became
The universe at once
While the others fled.
And one—

Not our universe—
Became something else.
Don't think about it
And you won't.

The landmass of the continental
United States compared to an open
Manhole
On the bitter boulevard where citizens buy crack

Is how much bigger the human brain is
Than the entire universe was at the start,
When it was the prickle
Before the zit.

Godspeed, John Glenn.
Fly safely high
In your seventy-seven-year-old
Head thirteen billion years old.

ETERNITY

A woman waits on a distant star she is traveling to.
She waits for herself to arrive.
But first she has to embark.
3, 2, 1 . . . ignition.

All systems are go for the facelift.
Her face lifts off into space.
She heads for the distant star
And the young woman waiting for her there.

A man who wanted to look better
But not younger is red
Swells of raw.
Later they will remove the staples.

Ten weeks later
They are younger.
They pull over
Their head a sock of skin.

One day the girl sees in the mirror a girl
Laughing so hard her face falls off in her hands.
You can see the inside of the face.
The front of her head is an amputee's smooth stump.

Her old woman's body is a bag of spotted slop.
The gentleman at least is doing fine.
His face peeks through the shower curtains
Of his previous face.

In the tomb air
Of the spacecraft they get more perfumed
As they painstakingly near
The hot banks of the Nile, so green and fertile.

Heart is safe in a dish of preservative.
Face is a box for the telemetry for the journey.
Perishable slaves caravan the monumental blocks of stone to the site.
The faceless likeness deafens the desert.

THE MASTER JEWELER
JOEL ROSENTHAL

What's Joel
Got to do but let the jewel
Hatch
The light and hook

It to the flesh
It will outlast
And point the staring
Woman at a mirror?

The stone alone was fireworks
But is Star Wars in his choker.
Of course Joel wears no jewelry himself but
Makes it for these reasons rhyme.

The staring woman is starving and
Eating her own face and
Stares with a raving smile
At her undying love.

The things they
Have to have
Are his
Designs on them.

The richest in the world stick out their necks
And hands and ears for JAR's gems—
Which they can ride through the eye of a needle
To heaven. His genius is his

Joy, is JAR, is
Agonized obsession, is death is double-parked
Outside the palace. Death is loading in the van
The women and camels of King Solomon it is repossessing.

Joel has designed a watch
In platinum.
This watch is the sequel
To anyone you have ever lost.

IN SPITE OF EVERYTHING

I had a question about the universe
On my way to my evening class,
Stuck between stations on the No. 3 Express,
And it was this.

You don't know what you mean
And that's what I mean.
God is playing peekaboo,
Not There behind the hands.

Then peekaboo and you
See face-to-face and bam.
I'm getting old.
I hid and I revealed myself.

All the way down to the wharf
All the way down to the wharf
All the way down to the wharf
He-wolf and she-wolf went walking.

Shut up, darling! I'll do the talking.
All the way down to the wharf
All the way down to the wharf
The stalker was stalking.

The talker was talking.
You want to talk
Until I droop.
The river runs by

Under the broken pier.
All the great ocean liners left for France from here,
Whose passengers are
Now ghosts mostly. Loup and Louve howl

To Neptune from their heaving gale-force stateroom—
Walk through drought, walk through dew,
Keep walking down the avenue,
For richer for poorer, for better for worse, malgré tout.

52 SPRINGTIME

Sunset rolls out the red carpet
For Charlotte as she walks
To her appointment with life
In the awed soft-focus.

Charlotte sees the crimson trees
With her famous eyes.
Fat rises to the surface of the street in sunset flames.
The magnolias are vomiting brightness

In the mist. Spring in its mania refuses
To take its medication. It
Buys every newspaper left on the newsstand, then
Sobs in a café, sobs with laughter.

A car at a light rocks from side to side with the
Windows down, letting in red, letting out rhythm—
A pounding pulse of rap from the exophthalmic car radio.
She would give anything to be able to

Sleep in a shower of this fragrance.
She is talking on her fear
Phone to anyone in her mind. She is
Saying in a red city

I am alive at sunset.
Charlotte is beautiful but
Charlotte is so beautiful it is
Insolence.

A fan
Asks for her autograph outside a restaurant.
Horse carriages slowly carry
Honeymooners through a fog of love as thick as snow.

A slave to love
Kisses a real slave she bought to free.
The dominatrix is whipped by her slave—
Who has made a mistake on the new rug and wags.

SUMMER

Kitsy and Bitsy and Frisky and Boo
Stream by, memories of moist
Moss—green morphine—
On each bank of a stream.

Fronds as delicate
As my feelings present
Those summers.
You could drink the water you swam

In, clear, cold, sweet, but August,
But August in St. Louis,
But August and the heat
That slows the green smell of the lawns

To tar, lyric
Of humidity
That thickens to a halt, but sweet, that swells
Up, that you escaped to dreams

From. In one,
Beauty and kindness combined
To walk across a room.
The daughter of Colonel Borders, Kitsy,

Means God has found a way, walks in through a door.
The universe begins at once.
The stars erupt a sky
They can be stars in, that they can be

Unicorns in a pen in.
The perfect knight in armor to slay the fiery dragon
Has sex with it instead.
I wake from the dream in the dark.

I barely see above
The steering wheel at twelve years old.
The park at night is warm.
The air is sweet and moist and cool.

FALL SNOWFALL

54

The book of nothingness begins
At birth.
The pages turn and there
Is far.

There is far from where
They start.
The pages turn into
The book.

And everything and everyone and
What is happening
Is blood in urine.
Ask the trees

The leaves leave.
They are left.
They remove their wigs.
They turn themselves in.

They stand there blank.
The now falls
On the fields white.
The smell of wood smoke stares and

The no falls,
Radios
Of blank now
On the fields.

A black crow shakes the no off.
Merrily we
Go around circling
The drain, life is but a dream.

The doctors in their white
No
Fall
On the fields.

CHRISTMAS

My Christmas is covered
With goosepimples in the cold.
Her arms are raised straight
Above her head.

She turns around slowly in nothing but a
Garter belt and stockings outdoors.
She has the powerful
Buttocks of a Percheron.

My beautiful with goosepimples
Climbs the ladder to the high diving board
In her high heels
And ideals.

The mirror of the swimming pool is looking up at her
Round breasts.
She bounces up and down
As if about to dive.

In her ideals, in her high heels,
The palm trees go up and down.
The mirror of the swimming pool is looking up at her
Bikini trim.

The heated swimming pool mirror is steaming
In the cold.
The Christmas tree is on.
A cigarette speedboat cuts the bay in two.

It rears up on its white wake.
Ay, Miami!
Ninety miles away
Is Mars.

The cigarette smokes fine cigars,
Rolls hundred dollar bills into straws.
My Christmas
Is in his arms.

COSMOPOLITANS AT THE PARADISE

Cosmopolitans at the Paradise.
Heavenly Kelly's cosmopolitans make the sun rise.
They make the sun rise in my blood
Under the stars in my brow.

Tonight a perfect cosmopolitan sets sail for paradise.
Johnny's cosmopolitans start the countdown on the launch pad.
My Paradise is a diner. Nothing could be finer.
There was a lovely man in this town named Harry Diner.

Lighter than zero
Gravity, a rinse of lift, the cosmopolitan cocktail
They mix here at the Paradise is the best
In the United States—pink as a flamingo and life-announcing

As a leaping salmon. The space suit I will squeeze into arrives
In a martini glass,
Poured from a chilled silver shaker beaded with frost sweat.
Finally I go

Back to where the only place to go is far.
Ahab on the launch pad—I'm the roar
Wearing the wild blazer, black stripes and red,
And a yarmulke with a propeller on my missile head.

There she blows! Row harder, my hearties!—
My United Nations of liftoff!
I targeted the great white whale black hole.
On impact I burst into stars.

I am the Caliph of paradise,
Hip-deep in a waterbed of wives.
I am the Ducati of desire,
144.1 horsepower at the rear wheel.

Nights and days, black stripes and red,
I orbit Sag Harbor and the big blue ball.
I pursue Moby-Dick to the end of the book.
I raise the pink flamingos to my lips and drink.

SEX

The woman in the boat you shiver with
The sky is coming through the window at.
We will see.
Keep rowing.

You have
An ocean all around.
You are rowing on bare ground.
The greasy grassless clay is dead calm.

You love your life.
You love the way you look.
You watch a woman posing for you.
How awful for you. There's no one there.

Inside the perfume bottle life is sweet.
The glass stopper above you is the stars.
You smell the flowers,
Some far-off shore.

The slaves are chained in rows rowing.
The motion back and forth
Is the same as making love.
You fuck infinity and that takes time.

It's a certain way of talking to arthritis
That isn't heart disease or trust.
You can't remember why
Your hands are bleeding back and forth.

The thing about a man is that—
Is what?
One hand reaches for the other.
The other has a knife in it to cut the head off.

The fish flops back and forth
In the bottom of the boat.
The woman pulls the boat along
By its painter that the king slash slave is rowing.

 SONG

How small your part
Of the world is when
You are a girl.
The forests and deserts are full

Of the animals
We ride and eat
And the wind and the light
And the night,

But if you are
A girl you may
As well live in Boston
Or be a grain of white rice

Or be a fleck
Of mica in a sidewalk.
I wanted to have
A monocle and stick—

Put on my top hat,
And be a grain
Of radium,
And radiate a stadium with my act.

It's about holding
The wide-eyed bearded head of
Holofernes
Aloft. From the carrier deck

We climb to altitude
With an attitude, with
Our laser-guided bombs targeting
The white enormous whale.

We need the sperm oil to light
Our lamps, have to stop
The huge white life for whalebone stays to cage
Our corsets.

THE SEAL

What did the vomit of a god
Smell like? Like no one else
And there were clouds of it
In the White House.

It was an impeachable
U.S. bald eagle
Because it was barking and sporting
In the moisture like a seal.

Tubby smooth
Energy tube of seal seeks tender veal
For the White House mess and in a zoo
It smells like that.

To be slick
And sleek and swim
And in yours have hers,
Her hand, her heart.

Once it was a god,
Now they toss it fish
And watch it leap
And make it beg.

They're looking
At TV and look
It doesn't look that bad.
The ones from outer space are landing now.

A seal went out to play
In the middle of an enormous bay
All the cities surrounded,
The size of the Dust Bowl, as brown,

And sang of a 21st century that was lyrical
About effluents and landfill,
And set the presidential seal
On doing something about race and ass.

HER SONG

I am presenting
Myself to
You for the punishment
I preserve.

Sometimes you seem to
Understand I am
Banished.
I am the emptiness of

Bandages
That wrap
The mummy. My heart
I preserve in a dish—

It is a dog collar on all fours.
Inside is the
Eloquence
Emptied out.

Your hand
Starts to thunder,
Starts to rain much
Harder.

You raised your hand
To touch my cheek.
You saw my eyes
Go berserk.

It is the terror.
It asks you
To make it more.
Don't fall

In love
With me and I won't either.
Don't stop when
I say stop.

GREEN DRESS, 1999

You want
To change your name to be new
For the
Millennium so do.

The trumpet sounds
Your smile.
You soar just
Sitting still.

Flapping wings of a
Flamingo, clouds
Of my angina
Blossom darkly into dawn.

Sunset follows
While they play
The songs one wants
To hear. Your

Legs made of eleven
Kinds of heaven
Leap to
Where they want to go.

But I don't know
How long I have the
Future for.
In the jungle of

The body is the beating of the
Tom-tom.
Living dot com—
How many hits on your site?

If dance is what you do, the bar
Is where you go to
Work. If what you do is drink,
You also hit the heart.

LETTER TO THE EDITORS OF VOGUE

I'm seeing someone and
I really want to,
But I
Am stuck in glue.

I would go anywhere
To be near
The sky above
And smell the iodine

Wine of the port of Algiers,
Or for that matter the freezing
Nights on the dunes
Of the Sahara are blood

That you can drink till dawn
Under the terror of
Stars to
Make you blind.

I am drinking gasoline
To stay awake
In the midst of so much
Murder.

My daughter squeaks and squeaks
Like a mouse screaming in a trap,
Dangling from the cat who makes her come
When he does it to her.

Her killer goes out into
The streets to join his brothers
In the revolution
Who don't have jobs.

The *plastic* packed beautifully
Inside a tampons box that I carefully leave in the loo
At Café Oasis goes rigid and the
Unveiled meet God.

JAMES BALDWIN IN PARIS

The leopard attacks the trainer it
Loves, over and over, on every
Page, loves and devours the only one it allows to feed
It.

How lonely to be understood
And have to kill, how lovely.
It does make you want to starve. It makes an animal kill
All the caring-and-sharing in the cage.

Start with the trainer who keeps you alive
In another language,
The breasts of milk
That speak non-leopard. Slaughter them.

What lives below
The surface in a leopard will have to live above
In words. I go to sleep
And dream in meat and wake

In wonder,
And find the poems in
The milk
All over the page.

Lute strings of summer thunder, rats hurrying
Away, sunshine behind
Lightning on a shield of
Pain painting out happiness, equals life

That will have to be extinguished
To make way. The sound trucks getting out the vote
Drive the campaign song down every street.
Hitler is coming to Harlem.

Hitler is coming to Harlem! / There will be ethnic cleansing. /
A muddy river of Brown Shirts / Will march to the Blacks.
Happiness will start to deface
Pain on the planet.

ST. LOUIS, MISSOURI

You wait forever till you can't wait any longer—
And then you're born.
Somebody is pointing something out.
You see what I'm saying, boy!

Can't find a single egg at his debutant
Easter egg hunt and has to be helped.
Jewish wears a little suit with a shirt with an Eton collar.
Blood cakes on the scratch on your little knee.

Excuse me a minute.
The angel is black as a crow.
The nurse comes back in the room.
It shakes the snow from its wings.

The waterfall hangs
Down panting in the humidity.
The roar at the top of the world
Is the icebergs melting in pain.

Don't play on the railroad tracks.
It is so hot.
The tracks click before you hear the train
Which the clicks mean is coming.

British consuls posted to St. Louis in those days
Before air conditioning had to receive extra pay.
The Congressman with a bad limp was bitter.
They had operated on the wrong leg, made it shorter.

My father's coal yards under a wartime heavy snow.
The big blue trucks wearing chains like S/M love.
Blessed are the poor, for they will have heat this Christmas.
The tire chains/sleigh bells go *chink chink*.

The crow at the foot of the bed caws you
Were the Age of Chivalry and gave my family coal.
And when it was hot your ice trucks delivered
To the colored their block of cold.

HAMLET

The horsefly landing fatly on the page
And walking through words from left to right is rage.
It walks, stage right to left, across the stage.
The play is called *The Nest Becomes a Cage*.

I'm reading *Hamlet*, in which a bulging horsefly
Soliloquizes constantly, played by
Me. He's getting old, don't ask me why.
His lines are not familiar. Then I die.

I have been thinking, instead of weeping, tears,
And drinking everybody else's, for years.
They taste amazingly like urine. Cheers!
I tell you this—(But soft! My mother nears.)

You wonder how I know what urine tastes like?
I stuck my finger in a hole in a dike
And made the heart near-bursting burst. Strike
While it's hot. You have to seize the mike

And scream, "This is I! Hamlet the Dane!" True—
Too true—the lascivious iceberg you
Are cruising to, *Titanic*, is a Jew
Ophelia loved, a man she thought she knew.

One day I was bombing Belgrade, bombing Belgrade,
To halt the slaughter elsewhere, knowing aid
Arrives through the air in the form of a tirade
Hamlet stabs through the arras, like a man does a maid,

Only in this case it was the father of the girl,
Poor Polonius, her father. She is a pearl
At the bottom of a stream, and every curl
Of nothing but herself is drowned. I whirl

Around, and this is I! a fellow fanned
Into a flame. The horsefly that I land
On her has little legs—but on command
Struts back and forth on stage, princely, grand.

FREDERICK SEIDEL

I live a life of laziness and luxury,
Like a hare without a bone who sleeps in a pâté.
I met a fellow who was so depressed
He never got dressed and never got undressed.

He lived a life of laziness and luxury.
He hid his life away in poetry,
Like a hare still running from a gun in a pâté.
He didn't talk much about himself because there wasn't much to say.

He found it was impossible to look or not to.
It will literally blind him but he's got to.
Her caterpillar with a groove
Waits for love

Between her legs. The crease
Is dripping grease.
He's blind—now he really is.
Can't you help him, gods!

Her light is white
Moonlight.
Or the Parthenon under the sun
Is the other one.

There are other examples but
A perfect example in his poetry is the what
Will save you factor.
The Jaws of Life cut the life crushed in the compactor

Out.
My life is a snout
Snuffling toward the truffle, life. Anyway!
It is a life of luxury. Don't put me out of my misery.

I am seeking more Jerusalem, not less.
And in the outtakes, after they pull my fingernails out, I confess:
I do love
The sky above.

AREA CODE 212

I do
Standing still.
I do in my head.
I do everything to keep active.

Everything is excellent.
I do pablum. I do doo-doo. I do heroic deeds.
I do due
Diligence.

I do heroic deeds. I don't move.
I do love
The sky above
Which is black.

I do white gloves at the dances,
But I don't dance with the fascists.
I do beat and smash their stupid wishes.
I take you to be my.

The river is turning into
A place to drown.
The road lay down
In front of the car.

Everything in hell was
Talking English long ago.
I mean English.
I mean fruit bowl. I mean upper crust. I mean, really!

The ocean swings back into view in inland St. Louis.
The time is then.
My headmaster's exotic psychotic wife goes completely
Round the bend and maintains

The Mississippi is down there and up here
Is Berchtesgaden. I am shooting up on this.
Breast milk leaks from the insertion point.
His wife—my bride—wanders around the campus saying I do.

THE BATHROOM DOOR

Decapitated, he looks much the same,
The same homeless mind.
He watches a starving man
Eating his hiccups

Because he has nothing else to eat
In front of the mirror that is
Brushing his teeth.
Then he goes to bed headless. Then

He hears his wife get out of their bed
And lock the bathroom door
That they never lock.
Both of them are drunk.

He sleeps with his eyes shut in the dark
For a few minutes and then he gets up.
But he doesn't get up.
She comes back to bed.

She says I am so afraid.
She says I feel cold.
He asks her what she has done.
He makes her stand up and walk. He calls 911.

He will go to the theater
Of the locking of the bathroom door, hiccup
Click, and how he stayed in bed
For the rest of his life.

He remembers something else.
That he did get up. He stood
Outside the door.
He went back to a bed

Even more terrible than the loyal eyes
Of a dog about to be euthanized.
Than the efforts of a racehorse
Who will have to be shot to rise.

DOWNTOWN

Think of the most disgusting thing you can think of.
It is beautiful in its way.
It has two legs.
It has a head of hair.

It goes downtown.
It goes into an art gallery.
It pulls out a gun.
It kills its friend.

Never mind how much money they made.
Start thinking about what matters.
The MV Agusta motorcycle
Is the most beautiful.

I Do was one.
The Bathroom Door was another.
I Do was one.
Pulled out a gun and fired.

It was point-blank.
It died instantly.
The fragment was Sappho.
You can imagine how beautiful.

The person is walking
Ahead of you on the sidewalk.
You see its back but its face
Is facing you as it walks away.

As if the neck were
Broken, but the face is calm.
The name of the face you
Face is the United Nations.

It is a lovely Picasso walking away
On a broken neck and looking straight ahead back.
First came the seen, then thus the palpable
Elysium, though it were in the halls of hell.

THE SERPENT

Who is this face as little
As a leaf,
The neck a stem?
The furnace waits.

Someone is happening
To someone. Someone is
Alive and enters
Defiantly.

Her lips are full.
The mouth is open.
The living room is full
Of mahogany and art.

The serpent concentrates its gaze until the serpent is
A sumo wrestler agile as a dragonfly,
A furnace eating only good
To stay big.

The girl is a delicate
Drop.
The beautiful face
Is a leaf.

The dragonfly
Practices touch-and-go landings
At the little airport, landing to take off,
See-through with heartbeats.

The serpent is not a serpent
But a lyre.
It asks to play.
It asks the girl to let a dragon fly.

Someone is sailing clay pigeons
And blowing them apart perfectly.
Someone is kissing
The other.

GETAWAY

I think you do
But it frightens you.
I have the guns
In the car.

I wanted to save
Someone and
The rest. It will happen.
I will take you hostage.

Also I wasn't
Going to fall in love
But when you're fleeing
You're flying.

Someone had to take
My blindfold off for me to
Just take off. I turn the key in your ignition.
Contact! The propeller flickers.

We are taking off to
Elope.
Have another
One

For the road. Burn the birth certificates.
Run the roadblock.
All the whirling lights
On the roofs of their cars.

They're going to check
The trunk and find our bodies.
I won't.
We jump out firing.

I am already in you.
I am rafting down your bloodstream.
That is already over.
I have entered.

NOTHING WILL

Root canal is talking
To the opposite—
Twenty-three years old,
With eyes like very dilated

Dewdrops sideways.
Age is visiting
The other side of the moon,
When the moon was young.

Wow, to see the side
That never faces the earth is cool,
And kiss newborn skin
That you could eat off of.

A clean twenty-three-year-old
Heart is tourism
For the senator
Visiting the strange.

You fly there, then get out and walk.
The space shot lands
And he gets out and flies and then on foot.
He is looking at her tits.

The future will not last.
It is coming towards her
On safari
To watch the ancient king of the savannah roar and mate

Despite a root
Canal spang in the middle.
Nothing will.
Not even root canal. Revive his satrapy.

He is rowing down a canal
Of Royal Palms on either side
And the ocean is near. The oil spill is near
Enough for her to hear it greasing the shore.

7 pH 3

Phineas has turned
To face the quiet Phoebe to
Touch her cheek.
Phineas, who is tender but not meek,

And certainly is not weak,
Is also not named Phineas.
The name is art.
Phineas turns to touch her tenderly,

But the cab runs over a
Pocked-moon stretch of Brooklyn roadway
And his hand is knocked
Into being a brute.

What is the pH of New York?
PH is
Singing to PH,
Date palm to date palm.

The dunes in every
Direction tower.
Their color is octoroon
In Manhattan at dawn.

That is the color
Of the heart they share
Which is an oasis
Where one can pause

Before going out to die
In the dunes,
Strangling without water
And without a gun

To shoot at night at the stars.
For the moment, they sing.
The saddle has no camel under it.
They know.

VENUS

Venus is getting
Smaller.
Finally, she is
The size of a mouse.

A fully developed young woman
That size
Makes it difficult
To caress her breasts.

The curly wire
To a Secret Service agent's ear
Ends in a plug actually bigger
Than her derrière.

What a magnificent goddess!
And enormous—when
She stands on the back of your hand
With her glorious assets!

Her steatopygous ass
Sticks straight out—a Hottentot harvest moon!
Her breasts are prodigious.
Her ass is steatopygous.

Her head is
Classically small.
Her eyes and her mouth
Are equally oceans and drops from a dropper.

Venus shrank down
To go to Harvard, and got a tiny degree.
Her Junoesque figure
Is the size of a sea horse.

Mr. Universe
Is in love,
But how will he get in?
Venus, goddess, tell him how!

NIGRA SUM

I'm having a certain amount of difficulty
Because I am finding it hard.
It is all uphill.
I wake up tired.

It is downhill from here.
The Emancipation Proclamation won't change that.
Evidently there have been irregularities apparently.
It is time to get out.

I am going to go public with this
Beautiful big breasts and a penis
Military-industrial complex.
I live in the infield with other connoisseurs

Behind the bars of the gate to the circuit,
Sniffing burning racing oil till I'm high.
On the other side of the gate is the start/finish,
And the red meat of the racebikes raving to race.

I'm not from anywhere. I'm from my head.
That's where I didn't grow up
And went to school.
Oh, I am totally vile and beautiful!

A military-industrial complex with soul!
Nigra sum sed formosa.
I am black but comely,
O ye daughters of Jerusalem:

Therefore has the king loved me, and brought me into his
Chambers. For, lo, the winter is past,
The rain is over and gone:
Rise up, my love, my fair one,

And come away.
Tomorrow I set sail for the bottom, never to return.
The master cabin has its own head—which I'm from.
I'm from my head.

RAIN IN HELL

That was the song he found himself singing.
He heard a splash before he hit the concrete.
There was no water in the pool.
He couldn't stop himself in time.

One day, while he was waiting for the light to change,
And suddenly it began to rain,
And all at once the sun came out,
He saw a rainbow of blood.

He was so excited.
Splash.
That he dove off
The diving board without a thought.

There was no water in the pool.
He heard a splash
Just before he hit the concrete.
Gosh—

From good in bed
To as good as dead!
You smell the rain before it comes.
You smell the clean cool pierce the heat.

He has the air-conditioning on
But keeps the car windows open driving back to town.
It is the story of his life.
He smells the rain before it falls.

It was the middle of the night
In 212, the Area Code of love.
The poem he was writing put
Its arms around his neck.

Why write a poem?
There isn't any rain in hell
So why keep opening an umbrella?
That was the song he found himself singing.

DIDO WITH DILDO

The cord delivers electricity
From the wall socket to my mouth
Which I drink.
I want you all to know how much

My hair stands on end.
You will leave me alive.
You will leave me and live.
I hold midnight in my hand.

The town siren sounds because it's
Noon. The sunlight throws spears
Into the waves
And the gulls scream.

You get there.
Something instantly is wrong.
It only seems it's instantly.
It always is

The case that different time zones
Produce
Different midnights.
I hold a new year in my hand.

She stood on her toes to kiss me
Like in the nineteen fifties.
I glued my mucho macho lips to destiny.
I hurl a fireball at the logjam.

I turn on the TV.
I turn the oven off.
I make a call on my cell phone
To the mirror.

I see in the mirror Aeneas
Has changed.
He is drinking vodka odorlessly.
Into Dido wearing a dildo.

I have a dream
And must be fed.
The manta rays when you wade out
Ripple toward your outstretched hand.

The answer is
The friendliness of the body.
There is no answer, but the answer is
The friendliness of the body

Is the stars above
The dock at night.
And in the afternoon lagoon flags lazily flap
Their bodies toward yours

To be fed. I landed on
An atoll in the soft
Perfume.
The airport air was sweet. The blond January breeze was young.

The windchill factor
Which is Western thought
Received an IV drip of syrup of clove.
I have a dream. I have a dream the

Background radiation is a
Warm ocean, and a pasture for
Desire, and a
Beach of royal psalms.

The IV bag is a warm ocean,
Is a body not your own feeding your body.
My body loves your body
Is the motto of Tahiti.

Two flying saucers mating,
One on top the other, flap and flow, in love.
Each is a black
Gun soft as a glove.

FEBRUARY

The best way not to kill yourself
Is to ride a motorcycle very fast.
How to avoid suicide?
Get on and really ride.

Then comes Valentine's Day.
It is February, but very mild.
But the MV Agusta is in storage for the winter.
The Ducati racer is deeply asleep and not dreaming.

Put the pills back in the vial.
Put the gun back in the drawer.
Ventilate the carbon monoxide.
Back away from the railing.

You can't budge from the edge?
You can meet her in front of the museum.
It is closed today—every Monday.
If you are alive, happy Valentine's Day!

All you brave failed suicides, it is a leap year.
Every day is an extra day
To jump. It is February 29th
Deep in the red heart of February 14th.

On the steps in front of the museum,
The wind was blowing hard.
Something was coming.
Winter had been warm and weird.

Hide not thy face from me.
For I have eaten ashes like bread,
And mingled my drink with weeping,
While my motorcycles slept.

She arrives out of breath,
Without a coat, blazing health,
But actually it is a high flu fever that gives her glory.
Life is death.

IN CAP FERRAT

God made human beings so dogs would have companions.
Along the promenade dogs are walking women.
One is wearing fur
Although the day is warm.

The fur
Trots behind a cur.
The mongrel sparkles and smiles
Leading her by the leash.

The month of March, that leads to hell,
Is plentiful in Cap Ferrat.
There is gambling around the bend
In the bay at the Casino in creamy Monte Carlo.

White as the Taj Mahal,
White as that stove of grief,
Is the cloud
Just passing by.

The air is herbs.
The sea is blue chrome curls.
The mutt sparkles and leers
And lifts a leg.

White as the weightless Taj Mahal,
White as the grief and love it was,
The day is warm, the sea is blue.
The dog, part spitz, part spots, is zest

And piss and Groucho Marx
Dragging a lady along.
The comedy
Is raw orison.

Dogs need an owner to belong to.
Dogs almost always die before their owners do.
But one dog built a Taj Mahal for two.
I loved you.

MARCH

He discovered he would have to kill.
He went to Paris to study how.
He returned home to throw out the colonial French.
He never left the United States.

He was a boy who was afraid.
He talked arrogance, secretly sick at heart.
He oozed haughty nonchalance, like a duke sitting on a shooting stick.
He grinned toughness on the playing field running behind his teeth.

He strutted in the school library, smirking
Like Charlie Chaplin twirling his cane jauntily.
He was a genius but he was afraid
He would burst into flames of fame and cry.

This Ho Chi Minh was arrogant. This Ho Chi Minh was shy.
Then he discovered poetry. It was in Florida
One March, at spring break, with his sister and parents,
Having parted for the week from his first girlfriend ever.

He wrote: *The sea pours in while my heart pours out—*
Words to that effect.
Even for age thirteen,
This was pretty dim.

This was the year of his bar mitzvah.
It was his genocidal coming of age in Cambodia.
Everyone who wore glasses was executed.
He took his off.

They killed everything in sight in a red blur.
It rained
A rainbow of the color red.
They wore black pajamas in a red bed.

They killed anyone named Fred.
This to start Utopia. Everyone was dead.
The Algerians blew up the French.
The French horribly tortured them to find out.

EASTER

The wind lifts off his face,
Which flutters
In the wind and snaps back and forth,
Just barely attached.

It smiles horribly—
A flag flapping on a flagpole.
Why is this idiot patriot
Smiling?

He is horribly
In love.
It is embarrassing to see
The red, white and blue.

The field of stars
Is the universe, his mind,
Which thinks about her constantly
And dials her number. *Hello. It's me.*

It really hurts
To see it in his face.
The awful smile of a dog
Is a grimace.

You can believe
In God again—God looks like him.
The Easter koan says the gas tank must be full
But empty. The taut wind sock

Sounds the trumpet,
Summoning all
To the new.
The trumpet sounds!

Sweet is spreading salt,
But only on the ice where people walk,
Only it is rice in slow motion showering fragrant
Spring rain on the couples.

A baby elephant is running along the ledge across
The front of an apartment building ten stories up.
What must be the young woman handler desperately gives chase,
Which has a comic aspect as she hangs on by the rope.

But the baby elephant falls, yanking the young woman floatingly
To her death on a ledge lower down.
The baby elephant lies dead on Broadway.
Every year it does.

Birds bathe in the birdbath in the warm blood.
The bed upstairs is red.
The sheets are red.
The pillows are blood.

The baby elephant looks like a mouse running away
Or a cockroach scuttling away on a shelf,
Followed by the comically running sandpiper
Holding the rope.

It is everywhere when you restart your computer.
You don't see it and then you do.
A half has already fallen to the street,
And the other is falling and hits the ledge.

Now is a vase of flowers
Maniacally blooming red.
The medallion cabs seem very yellow
Today—as yellow as lymph.

Every April 1st Frank O'Hara's ghost
Stops in front of the Olivetti showroom
On Fifth Avenue—which hasn't been there for thirty years.
He's there for the Lettera 22 typewriter outside on a marble pedestal

With a supply of paper—to dash off a city poem, an April poem,
That he leaves in the typewriter for the next passerby,
On his way to work at the Museum of Modern Art, because
The baby elephant is running along the ledge, chased by its handler.

A man picks up a telephone to hear his messages,
Returns the handset to the cradle, looking stunned.
The pigeon on the ledge outside the window
Bobs back and forth in front of New York City, moaning.

A man takes roses to a doctor, to her office,
And gets himself buzzed in, and at the smiling front desk
Won't give his name to the receptionist, just leaves red roses.
The doctor calls the man the next day, leaves a message.

There isn't anything more emptiness than this,
But it's an emptiness that's almost estival.
The show-off-ness of living full of May
Puts everything that's empty on display.

The pigeon on the ledge outside the window
Moans, bobbing up and down, releasing whiteness.
The day releases whiteness on the city.
And May increases.

Seersucker flames of baby blue and white
Beneath a blue-eyed Caucasian sky with clouds
Fill up the emptiness of East Side life
Above a center strip that lets red flowers grow.

They call them cut flowers when they cut them.
They sell the living bodies at the shop.
A man is bringing flowers to a doctor,
But not for her to sew them up.

And May is getting happy, and the temperature is eighty.
And the heart is full of palm trees, even when it's empty.
The center strip migraine down Park Avenue sees red.
Girl with a Red Hat in the Vermeer show is what it sees.

Vermeer went in a day and a half from being healthy to being dead.
A city made of pigeons is moaning in a morgue that's a garden.
The red hat reddens the Metropolitan.
It's its harem.

VENUS WANTS JESUS

Venus wants Jesus.
Jesus wants justice.
That one wants this.
This one wants that.

I want.
It means I lack.
Working men and women on
May 1st march.

They want to increase
The minimum wage and they will form a line.
My fellow glandes march
Entirely

Around the girl while
Around the world bands
Are playing.
On the White House lawn, "Hail to the Chief"

Greets the arriving helicopter slowly curtsying
On the landing pad.
They ought
To wait till the rotor stops. The president

Descends
The stairs waving. Behind him is
The uniformed aide with the attaché case carrying
The codes.

The president
Can place a lei around
A billion necks
In an hour.

They wanted to live till June.
They wanted the time.
They wanted to say goodbye.
They wanted to go to the bathroom before.

MV AGUSTA RALLY,
CASCINA COSTA, ITALY

Each June there is a memorial Mass
For Count Corrado Agusta in the family church,
Whose factory team of overwhelming motorcycles
Won every Grand Prix championship for years.

The courtyard in front of the sinister stark house
Where Corrado was raised blazes with victory.
The charming young choir in the tiny church sings,
To the strumming of a guitar, that other glory story.

In her MV Agusta T-shirt, the reader reads aloud the lesson.
The roaring of a lion about to devour her
Is an MV 500cc GP racer getting revved up for the rally:
The caviar and flower of Grand Prix four-stroke power.

The champions have no idle, so not
To die they have to
Roar. They roar like the lions in the Coliseum.
They roar like a pride of blood-red hearts in the savannah.

Someone blips
The throttle of the three-cylinder
500, one kind of sound, then someone pushes into life
The four. Its bel canto throat catches fire.

The priest elevates the Host
And his bored theatrical eyes,
To melodramatize the text,
Roar.

It's like the Mass they hold in France
To bless the packs of hounds before a hunt.
The choir of hunting horns blares bloodcurdling fanfares
And lordly stags answer from all the forests around.

I stand in the infield with other connoisseurs near tears
Behind the bars of the gate to the track, smelling burning castor oil.
On the other side of the gate is the start/finish line,
And Monica Agusta standing with her back to me, close enough to touch.

Eternal life begins in June.
Her name is fill the name in.
My contubernalis, my tent mate,
My woman in the tent with me in Latin.

The next world is the one I'm in.
My June contubernium.
My tent mate through the whole campaign.
The June moon, burning pure Champagne,

Starts foaming from its tail and rising.
One minute into launch and counting.
The afterlife lifts off like this.
The afterlife begins to blast.

The breathing of my sleeping dog
Inflates the moonlit room with silence.
The afterlife begins this way.
The universe began today.

The afterlife is here on earth.
It's what you're doing when you race
And enter each turn way too fast
And brake as late as possible always.

Of course the world does not exist.
A racebike raving down the straight
Explodes into another world,
Downshifts for the chicane, brakes hard,

And in the other world ignites
The flames of June that burn in hell.
My contubernalis, my tent mate.
My woman in the tent with me does octane.

Ducati racing red I ride,
Ride red instead of wrong or right.
The color red in hell looks cool.
In heaven it's for sex on sight.

JUNE ALLYSON AND MAE WEST

In the middle
Of the field of vision
Is a hole that is
Surrounded by a woman.

The hole is life.
The ones who are
About to be born
Have no choice.

The hole is life.
The ones who are
About to be born
Have no choice.

In the middle
Of the field stood
The middle of the light
Which is love, a heart of light.

I got better.
I can remember taking
A streetcar.
It was June.

The name of the movie star was June
Allyson who was with me in my hospital room.
I bet the glorious wicked star Mae
West would.

June made Mae good.
Mae made June bad.
Is it bearable?
The situation is

No one ever gets well.
People can't
Even stand up.
They pay to cry.

 JULY

Phineas is crossing the Pont des Arts,
But he is doing it in New York.
He has made up the Phineas part.
That is not his name.

Nothing is.
Nothing is his.
He is living in Paris,
On Broadway.

Two minutes from his door
Is the Pont des Arts arcing
Over the Seine.
Bateaux mouches like bugs of light

Slide by at night under his feet, fading away in English.
Shock waves vee against the quais.
Mesdames and gentlemen, soon we have Notre-Dame.
The letter *P* is walking across the Pont des Arts.

Back in New York,
Except he *is* in New York,
He is in Paris.
He strolls home to the rue de Seine, punches in the code and goes in.

The next morning the streets
Are bleeding under his feet.
They are cleaning themselves.
Apparently, they are not that young.

The trees are green.
In the Jardin du Luxembourg he says her name.
He watches the children riding the donkeys on the red dirt.
An adult holds the halter and walks alongside.

One tree is vomiting and sobbing
Flowers.
The smell is powerful.
How quatorze July it is to be a donkey and child.

HUGH JEREMY CHISHOLM

With Jeremy Chisholm at the Lobster Inn on our way to Sagaponack,
Eating out on the porch in the heat, flicking cigarettes into the inlet.
We ate from the sea and washed it down with Chablis,
Punctuated by our unfiltered Camels, in our eternal July.

Billy Hitchcock landed his helicopter at a busy gas station
In Southampton July 4th weekend, descended from the sky like a god
To buy a candy bar from the vending machine outside,
Unwrapped the candy bar and flew away, rotors beating.

Chisholm found a jeweler to paint his Tank Watch black.
It had been his father's, one of the first Cartier made.
The gold case in blackface was sacrilege.
Chisholm wore it like a wrist corsage.

In a helicopter that belonged to the Farkas family,
The carpet of cemeteries seemed endless choppering out to J.F.K.
So much death to overfly! It could take a lifetime.
They were running out of cemeteries to be dead in.

Hovering at fifteen feet,
Waiting for instructions on where to land,
Told to go elsewhere,
We heeled over and flew very low, at the altitude of a dream.

Bessie Cuevas had introduced me to this *fin de race* exquisite
Who roared around town in his souped-up Mini-Minor,
Who poured Irish whiskey on his Irish oatmeal for breakfast,
Who was as beautiful as the young Prince Yusupov

Who had used his wife as bait to kill Rasputin and, later in Paris,
Always in makeup, was a pal of the Marquis de Cuevas, Bessie's dad.
Yusupov dressed up a pet ape in chauffeur's livery
And drove down the Champs-Élysées with the ape behind the wheel.

WASPs can't get lung cancer smoking Camels,
Chisholm said, taking the usual long deep drag—look at cowboys!
That July they found a tumor
As big as the Ritz inoperably near his heart.

Sky-blue eyes,
A bolt of lightning drinking
Skyy vodka,
A demon not afraid of happiness,

Asks me about my love life here in hell.
I lunge at what I understand I belong to.
I flee, too.
It's her fate. It's too late.

I see the sky from a couch at the Carlyle.
Blond is dressed in black.
It all comes back.
The sky is black.

Thunder violently shakes
The thing it holds in its teeth
Until it snaps the neck
And rain pours down in release and relief,

Releasing paradise,
The smell of honeysuckle and of not afraid of happiness.
Lightning flashes once
To get the sky eyes used to it,

And then flashes again
To take the photograph.
The blackout startled her and started it.
Lightning flickers in Intensive Care.

I am speaking in Ecstatic.
The couch is floating on the carpet.
The waiter burns
From all the discharge and surge, and brings more drinks.

Coition is divine human
Rebirth and ruin having drinks in a monsoon,
In the upholstered gallery outside the bar, in the gold light.
The Prince of Darkness dipped in gold is God.

SEPTEMBER

The woman is so refined.
The idea of refinement gets redefined.
Doing it with her is absurd.
Like feeding steak to a hummingbird.

Her hair colorist colored her hair gold
To give her a look. It made her look cold.
Her face suddenly seemed see-through like a breath
In a bonnet of gold and she was in a casket and it was death.

She looked more beautiful than life.
She said she wanted to be my wife.
She comes with a psychiatrist to maintain her.
She comes with a personal trainer.

The September trees are still green in Central Park
Until they turn black after dark.
The apartments in the buildings turn their lamps on.
And then the curtains are drawn.

One person on a low floor pulls the curtain back and stares out,
But pulls the curtain closed again when there's a shout,
Audible on Fifth Avenue, from inside the park.
Somewhere a dog begins to bark.

I climb into the casket of this New York night.
I climb into the casket of the curtained light.
I climb into the casket and the satin.
I climb into the casket to do that in.

Into her roaring arms, wings of a hummingbird,
A roar of wings without a word,
A woman looking up at me and me looking down
Into the casket at the town.

I see down there His Honor the Mayor
In St. Patrick's Cathedral, head bowed in prayer.
His friend—wings roaring—hovers beside him in the pew.
Death is all there is. Death will have to do.

THE TENTH MONTH

Someone is wagging a finger in her face—*Charlotte!*
Down here in hell we don't do that!
As if she were a child. Charlotte has arrived
To test the torture.

This is a test. This is only a test. Charlotte
Is yelling at Charlotte for a violation.
Charlotte, as a Human Rights Watch
Observer of sorts, has descended from heaven to an early fall.

Oh dear, is it really October?
Is Charlotte really nearly over?
She still says actress—most actresses today would call themselves
An actor. A star walks down upper Broadway being beautiful

With her famous eyes. *Hello from hell,*
She tells her cell phone.
She's ready to hand
Down the indictments and waves her wand.

The crimes sparkle in the moonlight.
Actually, it's rather wonderful to stalk
The Upper West Side midday,
Between the Hudson River and Central Park,

Looking for a self to put the handcuffs on.
It's lovely if there's been a human rights violation.
There's also cruelty to animals,
The child pornography of do-gooders.

The animal is strapped down for the vivisection, conscious,
Buying a book in Barnes & Noble, pursued by fans
Telling her they love her movies here in hell,
And would she do it to herself for them again.

A man comes to the tenth month of the year and calls it Charlotte—
I don't believe in anything, I do
Believe in you. You always play
A garter-belted corpse of someone young.

FALL 94

It is
A hole surrounded
By a voluptuous
Migraine.

It was a universe that could
Burst out
And start
Without a trace

Of where it came from.
The background radiation
Is what's
Left of

The outburst at the start.
The background radiation
Is the delicious
Migraine. The hole of life

Is about to
Start.
Don't make sense.
It is about to start again.

Umbrellas pop open.
Mushroom caps approach a newsstand.
The trees wear truth and rouge.
The trees start to sing

In the soft.
The old penis smells food
And salivates.
One hundred ninety horsepower at

The crank
Going two hundred miles an hour down the straight
Is another motorcycle death
From Viagra in October.

OCTOBER

It is time to lose your life,
Even if it isn't over.
It is time to say goodbye and try to die.
It is October.

The mellow cello
Allée of trees is almost lost in sweetness and mist
When you take off your watch at sunrise
To lose your life.

You catch the plane.
You land again.
You arrive in the place.
You speak the language.

You will live in a new house,
Even if it is old.
You will live with a new wife,
Even if she is too young.

Your slender new husband will love you.
He will walk the dog in the cold.
He will cook a meal on the stove.
He will bring you your medications in bed.

Dawn at the city flower market downtown.
The vendors have just opened.
The flowers are so fresh.
The restaurants are there to decorate their tables.

Your husband rollerblades past, whizzing,
Making a whirring sound, winged like an angel—
But stops and spins around and skates back
To buy some cut flowers in the early morning frost.

I am buying them for you.
I am buying them for your blond hair at dawn.
I am buying them for your beautiful breasts.
I am buying them for your beautiful heart.

NOVEMBER

I've never been older.
It doesn't.
I can't explain.
Every November is one more.

I've used up my amount.
I've nearly run out.
I'm out of penis.
I've run out.

I look out the spaceship's vast
Expense of greenhouse glass
At the stars.
It will take a million years.

You open your head.
You look in the dictionary.
You look it up.
You look at the opposite.

You open the violin case.
You take it out.
Actually, it is a viola.
Actually, it is November.

You grab the handrails with the
Treadmill speeding up.
Oh my God. Don't stop.
It is possible that

The president traveling in an open limousine
Has been shot.
My fellow Americans, ask not
What your country can do for you in

November. The doorman
Holds the door.
The taxi
Without a driver pulls up.

GOD EXPLODING

They all claim responsibility for inventing God,
Including the ruthless suicides who call themselves God Exploding.
All the rival groups, of course, immediately take credit
For terrorist atrocities they did not commit.

One of the terrorist acts they did not commit
Was inventing rock 'n' roll, but, hey,
The birth of Elvis/Jesus is as absolute as the temperature
Of the background radiation, 4°K.

1, 2, 3, 4—I sing of a maiden that is makeles.
King of alle kinges to here sone che ches.
He cam also stille
Ther his moder was,

As dew in Aprille that fallith on the gras.
He cam also stille to his moderes bowr
As dew in Aprille that fallith on the flowr.
He cam also stille

There his moder lay,
As dew in Aprille that fallith on the spray.
Moder and maiden
Was never non but che;

Wel may swich a lady Godes moder be.
I hate seeing the anus of a beautiful woman.
I should not be looking. It should not be there.
It started in darkness and ended up a star.

Jewish stars on the L.A. freeway in Jewish cars
Take the off-ramp to the manger
Somewhere in the fields of Harlem,
Bearing gifts of gold and frankincense and myrrh.

Rock 'n' roll in front of the Wailing Wall and weep.
With the stump where your hand was blown off beat your chest.
Hutu rebel soldiers crucify the mountain gorillas.
Hodie Christus natus est.

THE WAR OF THE WORLDS

The child stands at the window, after his birthday party,
Gray flannel little boy shorts, shirt with an Eton collar,
St. Louis, Missouri, sixty years ago,
And sees the World Trade Center towers falling.

The window is the wall
The wide world presents to prepubescence.
People on fire are jumping from the eightieth floor
To flee the fireball.

In the airplane blind-dating the south tower,
People are screaming with horror.
The airplane meeting the north tower
Erupts with ketchup.

The window is a wall
Through which the aquarium visitors can see.
Airplanes are swimming
Up to the towers of steel.

Up to the Twin Towers to feed.
People rather than die prefer to leap
From the eightieth floor to their death.
The man stands at his childhood window saving them.

Old enough to undress himself,
Gray flannel little boy shorts, shirt with an Eton collar,
He stands at the worldwide window, after the birthday party,
And sees the mountains collapsing and collapsing.

On the other side of the aquarium glass is September 11th.
Under his birthday party clothes is his underwear and the underwater.
Why bother to wash your clothes, or your skin, why bother to wash,
When you will only get dirty again?

Why bother to live when you will die?
Visitors are peering through the thick glass and taking photographs
Of ground zero—of Allah akbar in formaldehyde in a jar.
God is great. Love is hate.

DECEMBER

I don't believe in anything, I do
Believe in you.
Down here in hell we do don't.
I can't think of anything I won't.

I amputate your feet and I walk.
I excise your tongue and I talk.
You make me fly through the black sky.
I will kill you until I die.

Thank God for you, God.
I do.
My God, it is almost always Christmas Eve this time of year, too.
Then I began to pray.

I don't believe in anything anyway.
I did what I do. I do believe in you.
Down here in hell they do don't.
I can't think of anything we won't.

How beautiful thy feet with shoes.
Struggling barefoot over dunes of snow forever, more falling, forever, Jews
Imagine mounds of breasts stretching to the horizon.
We send them to their breast, mouthful of orison.

I like the color of the smell. I like the odor of spoiled meat.
I like how gangrene transubstantiates warm firm flesh into rotten sleet.
When the blue blackens and they amputate, I fly.
I am flying a Concorde of modern passengers to gangrene in the sky.

I am flying to Area Code 212
To stab a Concorde into you,
To plunge a sword into the gangrene.
This is a poem about a sword of kerosene.

This is my 21st century in hell.
I stab the sword into the smell.
I am the sword of sunrise flying into Area Code 212
To flense the people in the buildings, and the buildings, into dew.

ONE HUNDRED

There was a door because I opened it.
It was the muse. It had a human face.
It had to have to make the three parts fit.
The Cosmos Poems was fire that filled the space

With fire in *Life on Earth*. The sky
Became a blue lake I was bathing in,
But it was fire. The sun was burning. Fly
Me to the bottom where I've been. I've been

Completing *Area Code 212*.
I've been in heaven in Manhattan on
The bottom. Hell is what to live can do.
One day I went downtown but it was gone.

The World Trade Center towers still return
In dreams and fall again and fall again
And rise again and people scream and burn
And jump to certain death again and then

They rise back to the hundredth floor and turn
Their cell phones on and call to say goodbye.
The firemen coming up the stairs will burn
Their way to heaven. Everyone will die

And perish, die and live. The people on
The top floors use their cell phones to call out.
Death follows birth as sunrise follows dawn.
High pressure sends a sky-high waterspout

Fire balances on top of. It begins,
The universe begins, and death begins,
And every living being burns and thins
Down to a flame that burns away and grins.

I heard them singing and set fire to it.
I hear their screams. Their corpses run in place.
They burst in flames to make the three parts fit.
My trilogy is fire that fills the space.

The muse now raised the laurel crown above
My corpse, and, praising me with what was fire
To hear, which I breathed in, which burned like love,
Now set ablaze the funerary pyre.

Dead white males greeted the arrival of
My ghost by praising me with what was fire
To hear, which I breathed in, which burned like love.
I wore the crown of laurel they require.

Beneath a crown of laurel lived a liar.
White man speak with forked tongue with his lyre.
They scream like gulls, beseeching. They scream higher
And dive down, crying, corpses on a pyre,

And rise back to the hundredth floor and turn
Their cell phones on. We call to say goodbye.
We firemen-coming-up-the-stairs will burn
Our way to heaven. Everyone will die.

You fling yourself into the arms of art.
You drool to sleep on consolation's shoulder.
A living donor offers you a heart.
The muse does. Yours got broken getting older.

The UFO that offers you the heart
Replacement is returning from out there,
Deep space, but beaming brain waves saying, Start
Down there, unsheathe the sword inside the ploughshare,

And cut the kindness from your chest, and stick
The Cosmos Poems in the cavity.
A hummingbird of flame sips from a wick.
My tinder drinks the lightning striking me.

Exploding fireballs vaporize the gore.
The runners-on-your-mark can't live this way.
They have to make the deal so they ignore
Their death and now the flames have come to stay.

They open windows. Now the brave begin
To lead the others to the stairs to die.
The money is the cosmic insulin
The partners in the firms must make. I fly

The UFO that offers you the heart
Replacement that's arriving from out there,
Its home, while down here the red mist is art
Exploding on the sidewalk from the air.

And some jump holding hands, but most alone,
But some jump holding hands with my warm hand.
They wait inside their offices. They phone
This poem. They stay and while they do they stand.

When I consider how my days are spent,
I'd have to say I spend a lot of time
Not being dead. I know what Garbo meant.
My life is life emerging from the slime

And writing poems. Virgil took my hand.
We started up the steep path to the crest.
He turned to warn me. Did I understand
I would be meeting Dante? I confessed

I hated cold. To flee the urban light
Pollution in the night sky and see stars
Meant getting to a crest of freezing blight
And human nature inhumane as Mars,

And things far stranger that I can't describe.
I greeted Dante. *Maestro!* Dawn neared. I
Was looking in the mirror at a tribe
In tribal costumes worshipping the sky.

It made no sense on Easter morning to
Parade in feathers down Fifth Avenue,
Except the natives worship what is true,
And firemen in white gloves passed in review.

The Jewish boy had done it once again.
Wood water tanks on top of downtown flamed.
The Resurrection has returned dead men
And women to the New York sky untamed.